RAISING
Good Kids

BACK TO FAMILY BASICS

DR. RAY GUARENDI

OUR SUNDAY VISITOR PUBLISHING DIVISION
OUR SUNDAY VISITOR, INC.
HUNTINGTON, INDIANA 46750

The "stand-alone" quotations from parents are excerpted from *Back to the Family: Proven Advice on Building a Stronger, Healthier, Happier Family*, by Dr. Ray Guarendi with David Eich (New York: Simon & Schuster, 1991). All rights reserved.

Every reasonable effort has been made to determine copyright holders of excerpted materials and to secure permissions as needed. If any copyrighted materials have been inadvertently used in this work without proper credit being given in one form or another, please notify Our Sunday Visitor in writing so that future printings of this work may be corrected accordingly.

Copyright © 2011 by Ray Guarendi. Published 2011.

16 15 14 13 12   2 3 4 5 6 7 8 9

All rights reserved. With the exception of short excerpts for critical reviews, no part of this work may be reproduced or transmitted in any form or by any means whatsoever without permission in writing from the publisher. Contact:

Our Sunday Visitor Publishing Division
Our Sunday Visitor, Inc.
200 Noll Plaza
Huntington, IN 46750

1-800-348-2440
bookpermissions@osv.com

ISBN: 978-1-59276-777-9 (Inventory No. T1082)
LCCN: 2010939230

Cover design: Amanda Falk
Cover photo: Shutterstock
Interior design: Dianne Nelson

PRINTED IN THE UNITED STATES OF AMERICA

To my grown-up children:
Stay close to God.

CONTENTS

INTRODUCTION

Great family life is not rocket science. The only thing that's rocket science is, well, rocket science. Great family life is firmly grounded on basics. "Proven new secrets to family success" are neither as proven as time-tested wisdom nor are they secrets. The only secret to raising good kids is that there are no secrets. Master some basics, and you'll be well on your way to a family that's as impressive as, well, rocket science.

> *"The single most important thing I'd write in a child-rearing book – chapter one, page one, first paragraph, first sentence – is that you get back what you put in."*
> DON (A FATHER IN CONNECTICUT)

What Are the Basics?

Time, communication, discipline, respect, morality. That's it? Who doesn't know these as strong family building blocks? True, there is no earth-shattering revelation here. Yet for most of us, the key to good living — family and otherwise — is not simply knowing what to do, but in doing what we know. That's where the real rocket science comes in.

CHAPTER 1

Quantity Time

Time is the framework upon which all other family success hangs. It takes time to talk out troubles. Time to discipline consistently. Time to convey, "You matter to me." It takes time and much repetition to teach character and morals. There are no shortcuts. If you skimp on time, you shortchange most everything else.

So how much time? Or more to the point, how does one find enough time, given other unyielding life demands? Let's consider a few basics of this basic.

Quality or Quantity?

I wonder if some career-driven expert somewhere conjured up the notion of quality time to compensate for his own dwindling home presence. The gist of quality time is this: It matters not so much how much time is spent with a child; what counts more is the quality of the time. Make sure what time you do share is interactive, enjoyable, rewarding. No doubt, all of these are positive goals. But speaking as one family-type expert, I wouldn't give the "quality versus quantity" debate the time of day.

Speaking as one family-type expert, I wouldn't give the "quality versus quantity" debate the time of day.

First, quality time resists scheduling. For that matter, so do kids. Neither fits neatly into a day planner. Or put another way, quality is much harder to negotiate without its partner: quantity. Quantity is the main medium of togetherness.

Second, despite what kids think, boring time is good time. You could say that it's even stimulating. It's a simple equation: The more downtime, the more uptime — whether it's an impromptu tickle fight, a "Dad, can I ask you something?" conversation, or a cutthroat game of "Twister." Maybe you'd better just observe this last one.

In our go-go, do-do, run-run society, home life is being forced to yield. We have devalued the currency — that is, the unscheduled hours from which spring the unexpected stuff of memories.

Rethink your activity schedule. Cut back, even eliminate, those "quality" pursuits that, while perhaps desirable in themselves, can accumulate and push aside the more valuable things of family. Don't chase the good at the cost of the best.

"It just seems to me that the quantity of time spent together increases the odds of those spontaneous quality times which everyone appreciates."

A MOTHER IN DELAWARE

Raise Your Profile

Despite what my kids think, this is not home life, circa 1884. The connection that occurred naturally as parents and children worked daily, side by side, is no longer the norm for the vast majority of us. More responsibilities and activities outside of family encroach upon the hours (minutes?) we have left to be with one another.

Rather than letting family time become another "event" or demand, "de-structure" some of it. The best moments aren't necessarily wrapped around playing blocks on the floor with a 4-year-old, or building a cardboard fort with a nine-year-old, or going jeans shopping with a 17-year-old. (Are you sure she wants you to?) Certainly these can be times well spent, but they are not the only measure of good family interaction. When asked about her best times with her own mother, one mother couldn't recall many particulars, just that her mother was "there in my life."

Call it "passive presence." It is the mere physical "nearby-ness" of a spouse to a spouse or a parent to a child. Are your kids watching a DVD in the family room? Read the paper there rather than in the kitchen (or if you're a dad, in the bathroom). Is your spouse cooking dinner? Do the bills at the kitchen table or counter rather than in the den. If your boys are outside playing (Do kids still do this? It isn't 1884, you know), you needn't always be the "steady pitcher." What if you sat outside and just watched?

When my older children were younger — and so was I — I played more than I observed. Now I find myself offering, "I'll be the ref. I can see best from my lawn chair on the deck." Actually, they never ask me to be the steady pitcher anymore. Something about not being able to throw strikes.

Our family has a tradition called "cuddle time." It's a movie with all of us huddled together in the family room. Recently, the kids picked something acceptable for all ages — always a requirement — and everyone watched, except one family member who fell asleep about eight minutes into it. I did last four minutes longer than my wife. The next day I told my son Sammy, "I'm sorry I cut out on you kids so fast." He sincerely replied, "That's okay. You were still there with us." I doubled his allowance.

As a young adolescent, I received organ lessons. My dad worked in a factory, often coming home tired. Some nights, sitting in the living room, he'd listen to me practice. As I slowly improved, note by note, he had requests. "Ray, play 'Spanish Eyes' for me." I sure do miss Pop in the audience, but he's there clearly in my memory. And no doubt his quiet listening to my hard-to-listen-to playing encouraged me to get skilled enough to later play professionally for ten years.

Passive presence. Being there. Keeping a higher profile. All of these are ways of saying that time together is sometimes just time side by side.

Group Eating

Survey after survey confirms the inestimable value of families eating meals together. One study touted it as the most common characteristic of families whose children did well academically. Again, as out-of-family pursuits gain weight, one of the first at-home routines to get swallowed up is mealtime. ("We'd like to, but it's just so hard with all the different schedules.") Okay, so the days of six-nights-a-week family dinners have faded rapidly since ... if not 1884, then 1984. Still, is there room to add a few meals to the weekly total? Some of this will occur naturally as a by-product of reducing hectic, overjammed existences. Some of it will require a deliberate decision to reorient the

If your family meals are events coming by as often as Halley's Comet, make the most of those you do have.

family schedule. If your family meals are events coming by as often as Halley's Comet, make the most of those you do have. Declare some "Rules of the Table":

- No technological noise allowed — no television, radio, or phone calls answered. It's probably just a telemarketer anyway; they still count on people being around home at dinnertime. And for heaven's sake, no headphones or text messaging. What's your 13-year-old doing with a cell phone anyway? Talk about a family-time thief!

- No one can leave the table until all are finished eating. This will be agony to the 12-year-old forced to sit and wait on a dawdling 6-year-old. Nonetheless, it should curtail the shovel-down-my-meal-so-I-can-get-elsewhere eating style that adolescents will perfect if you let them. To further torture the older ones, allow younger ones to share their stories too, no matter how disjointed, irrelevant, and rambling. Just don't interrupt them. They'll start over.

Meals are classic venues for "multiple-member passive presence." Sometimes not much direct interaction occurs other than "Can I have more bread?" With more regular meals, however, the presence becomes more active. The kids may ask for more carrots too. To borrow from the experts' cliché, your mealtime will evolve from quantity to quality — lots of it.

Play Some One-on-One

When grown children from strong families were asked to recall their best memories with Mom and/or Dad, many pointed to being with a parent one-on-one. While good times were had with the whole family, a unique warmth was expressed for the chance to do something or go somewhere with one parent, sometimes both. The sense of specialness arose from being the sole focus of Mom's and/or Dad's time and attention — not in an indulgent "Whatever you want, Princess, because you know I like you better than the others," but in a form of time undivided.

Dads, ask out a girl — your daughter. Call her at home. Set the time. Together, pick the activity — dinner, movie, miniature golf, oil-and-filter change (she may say she has plans already on this last one). Bring flowers. Little girls are still too young to be suspicious about what you did wrong. My wife has the antiquated notion that I not date other women, but she does approve of my keeping company with our daughters. Not much makes a girl feel more loved by Daddy than that.

"My parents always made me feel like I was somebody. They would sit patiently and listen while I stumbled through some stupid joke I heard at school, even though most times I blew the punch line."

MICHAEL (AN ADULT SON IN INDIANA)

My career involves some traveling. At one time, our ten children were aged 12 and under. As each became old enough to not continually embarrass me in public, one or two would come along with me on an overnight trip — hotel stay, sub sandwiches, snacks, late bedtime — the whole Disney Dad thing. Though I suspect I'd have to pay the older ones by the hour to accompany me now, they still talk about those days. The younger ones remain eager to be travel companions, so long as I keep the snacks coming.

Running errands? Take along a child. Require his company if you think best. Time together is far too important to be left always and only to a child's discretion. Visiting elderly Aunt Mary? She'd love to see one of the kids. She'll feel valued, and your child will learn a valuable lesson in compassion and virtue. Besides, Aunt Mary will probably give him a dollar. She has done this for years. The woman has no sense of inflation.

Watching TV? Rotate which child sits on the couch next to you. If he's reluctant, I've found that a bowl of chips in my lap attracts friends.

"Instead of 'quality time,' we planned 'equality time.' Since I spent more time with the baby, Ron [husband] spent extra time with big brother."
CANDY (A MOM IN ARKANSAS)

Take Away

Family time takes diverse forms. Not much is better than time showing a youngster she is unique, just like each of the others is.

CHAPTER 2

Stop, Listen, Talk

So much has been written, theorized, and hypothesized — in short, communicated — on how to interact adeptly with family that I'm kind of confused. Is my listening active or passive? Did I deliver a "you message" when an "I message" was called for? Is my positive-to-neutral statement ratio above 4.62, the minimum needed for maximum self-esteem formation? I'm trained in this communication stuff, experienced even, and sometimes I wonder: "How does one listen, and listen well?" As my wife accused me recently, "Ray, you're not listening to me." Or something like that, anyway.

Fortunately for me, and for you too, good communication is not complex, though some may seem to make it so. Practice a few fundamentals, and who knows? You could be as masterful as a professional psychologist. Do you hear what I'm saying?

Talking Begins With Listening

A passive action takes less effort than an active one. Listening is passive. It doesn't require much in the way of energy other than keeping quiet and staying attentive. Okay, maybe that's really hard for you. But it would seem easier in the long run than saying too much, too early.

> *"His thoughts were slow. His words were few.*
> *And never formed to glisten.*
> *But he was a joy to all his friends.*
> *You should have heard him listen."*
> AUTHOR UNKNOWN

Many arguments — between big people or between big and littler people — could be tempered, or even eliminated, if one party would just hold his tongue briefly. For spouses, a few minutes (seconds?) of silent focus on the other's words convey a loud message: "I'm waiting to hear more of what you have to say, even though I might not like it one bit." This is not to say that you can't respond. It is to say this: Delay the urge before you do. And when you do respond, you'll know more what you're talking about because you'll know more what your spouse is talking about.

Good listening, however briefly one can hold the pose, speaks respect. It says, "You matter. I'll give you your peace before I react, or worse, counterattack." It says, "I'm interested and willing to consider your words more than I'm itching to defend me." It says, "Keep talking. I'm just letting you get twisted up in your own illogic." All right, skip this last one — though it is tempting, isn't it?

For parents, quietly allowing, even for a minute or so, a youngster to wax eloquent in his own shortsightedness or childish perspective might seem like running a marathon one day after knee surgery. "Mom, I don't see why I can't stay out after 2:00 a.m. There's less chance to get into trouble because there are fewer people out. And the later, the better, because there are even fewer people around."

Now, how can you counter such flawless logic? Better to just remain silent, as a deer in headlights, and let Sherlock get all his thinking out in the open. After all, as long as he's going on, he's right in front of you. He can't follow through on his plans, not until tonight anyway. And when you finally do respond, chances are you'll speak with more credibility and authority — that is, unless you're so enraged that you can't see straight, much less talk straight. Either way, nothing is ever hurt by listening longer, and sometimes it actually helps.

A final point: You may hear, most commonly from an adolescent, "You don't listen to me." That does not automatically indicate you don't listen. Often it means "You didn't change your opinion to agree with mine." Listening in and of itself does not mean agreement.

Affection: Silent Love

Listening is wordless communication. It speaks volumes. Affection can also be wordless, and it speaks even louder. The best families are bilingual. They talk love in two languages: verbal and nonverbal.

As with all traits, the natural inclination to express affection varies wildly among people. Some struggle with the tiniest display of warmth. The story goes that a frustrated spouse was lamenting to her husband that for years she had been starving for the smallest crumb of an "I love you," to which he replied: "I told you that on our wedding day. If anything changes, I'll let you know."

The best families are bilingual. They talk love in two languages: verbal and nonverbal.

Even given such extreme reticence, in my clinical experience, nearly anyone can get better at showing warmth. For the above fellow, an "I love you" every two or three years would have constituted a relatively frenzied display of openness. Excepting those with some deep-seated discomfort with open affection, most people don't express warmth for one core reason: They've let the habit fade. They've taken for granted that others know how they feel, so why repeat themselves? To a lesser degree, they've come to resemble our wedding-day husband.

If you feel love, say it. If you don't feel love, not from lack but from laziness, say it anyway. If that proves too high an initial hurdle, say it nonverbally — a kiss, a hug, a touch, a tickle, a shoulder slap, a handshake, a playful wrestle, a hair tussle (not with teenage girls; they could hurt you).

Most loving people can say, "I do that." Okay, but how much? Like most conduct, if it's worth doing, it's worth doing more. As the philosophers advise: *Do the act; the feeling will follow.* In this case, the feelings will grow, for you and the recipient.

One study found that if a waitress gently touched a customer during their interaction, her tips rose significantly. If a stranger responds well — with money, no less — to touch, how much more would those we love? Who knows? Maybe you could quit work.

Affection needn't always be obvious. Sometimes a family code works. A mother of teens who was too expressive for her boys — in public, that is — insisted on giving them three subtle squeezes on the arm, signaling "I love you." She was happy. The boys were relieved, while still living in abject fear that one day she might slip, actually uttering those unspeakable words within another's earshot. Something tells me, though, that down deep, the boys loved their mom's way, ever more as they got older.

Not His Real Name

I've played amateur softball for over thirty years. Our roster of players has included John (Crybaby), Eric (Ebo), Mike (Mo-man), Thom (Grubber), Phil (Ragin'), Ron (Bish), Terry (Gib), and me (Hobbs). In fact, anyone who's played more than a few years with us has lost his birth name, to have it replaced by a team-dubbed one. Why all the name exchanges? They happen naturally, by-products of a familiar camaraderie.

You don't have to play softball to get and give a nickname. Families are an even better field for warm, sometimes colorful pet names. Nearly all soon-to-be parents, after agonizing throughout pregnancy over what to name their infant son or daughter,

Victoria becomes "Vittyboo." Sebastian becomes "Sea Bass." Andrew becomes "Android." It just happens, driven by a love that is growing faster than words can keep pace.

within three months post-birth have all but discarded the cultural common name for a one-of-a-kind one. Victoria becomes "Vittyboo." Sebastian becomes "Sea Bass." Andrew becomes "Androol." It just happens, driven by a love that is growing faster than words can keep pace.

Are pet names part of your family book? Probably. If not, form some. They are more than nominal signs of affection. A pet name is a steady reminder that someone is known closely and deeply.

Begin a Tradition

A tradition isn't necessarily centuries, or even decades, old. A tradition can be something done enough to become a valued part of someone or "someones." Traditions are the unique signature of a family, marks of one being connected to a bigger "us."

Traditions can be annual: the first-week-of-June beach trip, finding a Christmas tree the Sunday after Thanksgiving, or a husband buying a wife a brand-new dual-bag vacuum cleaner for Christmas. (On second thought, skip that last one. I tried it ... once.) Traditions can be monthly: a first-Sunday-of-the-month family breakfast out (or a kids-picked restaurant) or a Saturday-morning visit to the library to store up books for the month. Weekly: a Friday-night-at-home movie and popcorn. Daily: the piggyback ride to bed, complete with prayers, story, and tucking in. My daughter Liz thinks our family traditions are *nonnegotiable*, judging by how incessantly she nags for the next one.

Anything done regularly can rapidly become a tradition. The family knows it's predictable, anticipates it, and spends time talking about its details and how it should be structured. A tradition is people-glue. It forms memories. It helps solidify a family's identity: *This activity we share together is a reliable sign of who we are.*

It's All in the Timing

A national survey of strong families revealed this truth of good communication: The *when* matters as much as the *how*. Just as quality time resists being plugged into a prearranged schedule, so too does quality communication. Much of the good stuff of sharing isn't prompted; it occurs spontaneously. When the urge hits, kids, including teens, want to talk, even to us grown-ups, even if it's just because we're the only ones around.

There is a twelve-year span between the oldest and youngest of our ten children, five of whom are now teenagers. I've learned — my wife grasped it naturally —

25

that the "good talks" can erupt at anytime, anywhere, about anything. And I'd better be ready to put down my book, mute the TV (turning it off might be asking a bit much), stay awake a little longer, and postpone for a few minutes, in my mind, that all-consuming event or chore. As I look back, I see how easy it was to let those times of spontaneous "Dad, did you ever ..." or "Do you know what happened to me today?" skip by, as I was locked into my own thoughts or pursuits.

Sometimes "spontaneous" connections occur at regular times of the day. For younger children, bedtime is prime time to tell Mom or Dad everything, in agonizing detail, over and over, if just to stall the inevitable — having to sleep. Mealtimes, too, are made for sharing. Everybody is within ten feet of one another. Reciprocal talk will happen whether it's asked for or not. Surprisingly, chores done together make for another nice medium of exchange, even if at first only as a grumble session over child-labor laws being violated. How about short trips in the car, with one child, radio off, and no cell phone in use? Nighttime driving offers a sense of anonymity for the more delicate topics.

Headsets, as well as cell-phone texting, instant messaging, MyFace, or whatever, are conversation usurpers.

One more recommendation to enhance the probability of better, more

26

frequent communication: Dramatically limit headset wearing in the house, the car, or during family outings. Headsets, as well as cell-phone texting, instant messaging, MyFace, or whatever, are conversation usurpers. They'll steal countless moments of real-life communication. Don't let them take up unquestioned residence in your family residence. Keep them in their technological place. They have a way of crowding out other, better opportunities to be together.

Take Away

Listening well, expressing affection freely, communicating often — all are basic to raising good kids.

CHAPTER 3

Discipline:
Love in Action

Shaping morals and character — the foremost goal of nearly all parents — is difficult, if not impossible, without discipline. Rewarding "acceptable" behavior, arranging win-win scenarios, and maintaining a state-of-the-art sticker system will take you only so far. To raise an exemplary human being, you need discipline: high expectations backed by clear consequences. In the words of one veteran mother: "Discipline is love in action."

During the past few generations, unfortunately, discipline has taken a beating, primarily at the hands of child-rearing experts promoting fashionable, "kinder and gentler" theories. It isn't only the switch and hairbrush of Grandpa's day that's been thrown into the discipline dustbin. The ascending attitude in child-rearing circles is that discipline would best be a last resort. Psychologically savvy parents should be able to reason, persuade, reward, and emotionally guide their unruly charges into cooperation, into internalizing an attitude of "Oh my, Mother. Now I understand what you're saying. Of course I'll listen, because you're the much wiser grown-up who always knows what's best for me." I did hear a report once about a youngster

Discipline has taken a beating, primarily at the hands of child-rearing experts promoting fashionable, "kinder and gentler" theories.

who expressed something similar, but I never could get independent confirmation of its validity.

Said simply, modern notions of parenting have watered down discipline. Consider these words: authority, strictness, control. They seem to have a negative psychological tinge, don't they? Or worse, do they sound a bit Neanderthal? A brief "time-out" has replaced spanking. Win-win scenarios can erode a parent's authority. Sticker charts have supplanted the denial of privileges. In short, reliable, time-tested methods have increasingly been called into question by newer, more "enlightened" techniques.

It's not that such techniques in themselves are faulty. Certainly they can be part of any good discipline style. That said, trouble can arise if they form the backbone of a parent's authority. "Psychologically correct" approaches may sound swell on paper, but most real-life kids defeat them. Children by nature are too willful to respond well to discipline that isn't clear-cut, firm, and enforced at the hand of a confident parent.

> "My master's degree [is] in counseling, and ...
> when my oldest son turned 2 and started assert-
> ing himself, I burned my books and got out my
> wooden spoon."
>
> A MOTHER IN BOZEMAN, MONTANA

Discipline: Why?

When I was a young shrink in training — a "shrin-kling"? — I imbibed a load of parenting techniques. "Have tools, will travel" was my motto. As I counseled more parents, I was forced to conclude: Offering ideas is the easier part; the challenge lies in convincing a parent to implement these ideas. While most parents have a good sense of what makes for solid discipline, many have reasons that stay their hand. They're tired, or feel guilty or that they're being mean, or fear parenting "mistakes," or disagree with their spouse, or think their kids will rebel, or face a mother-in-law who already sees them as the nastiest witch/warlock to fly across the face of the earth.

No matter the resistance, one overarching reality rules: A loving parent is his child's kindest, most gentle teacher about life. Never again will that little person receive the unconditional love, the benefit of the doubt, or the forgiveness offered by a good parent (good spouses excepted). If a parent disciplines weakly today, the world will discipline strongly tomorrow. And the world hurts. If a child acts nasty, he sits on the couch. Brutal. If an adult acts nasty, he could get fired, punched, or have to sleep on the couch or in the basement. The stakes are higher as kids get older. To put it bluntly: *Don't let the world discipline your children.*

> *"Discipline without love may be harsh. Love without discipline is child abuse."*
> DR. RAY GUARENDI

Discipline — the Essence

What is discipline? Is it teaching? Is it training? Supervision? Rules? Consequences? It is all of these. But let's distill it to its essence, as understood by most people: DISCIPLINE **is establishing limits and expectations backed by consequences.** It is teaching a child: "If you do A, B will result, sometimes from life, sometimes from me." And it's a teaching that lasts for the better part of two decades.

Parents routinely ask, with some anxiety, "Can I be too strict?" My short answer: "No. Not when love flows around and through the discipline." My longer answer: "If *strict* means maintaining and enforcing high standards, not only for the children, but for all the family, it is hard to be too strict. On the other hand, if *strict* means loud, mean, or getting personal, yes, one can to be too strict."

Which leads directly to the great illusion of discipline: words. It's all too easy to confuse authentic discipline with its counterfeits: excess words, high volume, and nasty emotions. No matter what their form — nagging, negotiating, threatening, yelling — words are not discipline. They only lead to more words and more frustration.

Discipline is action. Discipline is doing something about a particular misbehavior. Warning Rocky sixteen times, with rising decibels per reiteration, to quit tormenting his brother is not sixteen pieces of discipline. It may sound so, and feel so. But it is sixteen pieces of talk. It is inaction. Making Rocky write twenty-five nice things about his brother is discipline.

Arguing with Oral every three hours about her incessant text messaging is not discipline. Confiscating her cell phone or limiting texts to five a day is. Maybe you could text her your new rule. She's more likely to get the message.

Discipline Law #101 asserts: Real discipline works and leads to less discipline. Imitation discipline is futile and leads to more and louder imitation discipline. In other words: Give them the *real* stuff. You, and they, will be glad you did.

> *"If you can get things going in a positive discipline direction, you won't have to chase after them endlessly in a negative direction."*
>
> A MOTHER OF SEVEN IN TILTON, NEW HAMPSHIRE

Discipline — Authority's Partner

Remember "the look"? Most parents of past generations had "the look," or some variant thereof — fingers snapping, throat clearing, paper rustling. By all measures, none of these "discipline" techniques should have worked. They weren't verbal, they held no consequences, and they were vague. Why, then, did they so often evoke cooperation, or at least a ceasing of *non*cooperation?

Simple — they signaled authority. They were a preliminary to action, an action that seldom had to occur. Why? Because early on, many of us learned that unpleasant consequences would befall us if we ignored, or challenged, "the look" or any other of our parents' discipline nonverbals.

Some parents still have "the look." Others tentatively experiment with it, only to receive a return look that says, "What are you looking at?" Kids haven't changed much. We grown-ups are the ones who've changed. As a group, we're just not as confident or authoritative as parents once were.

A parent will lament, "I can't understand it. I never would have treated my parents the way my daughter (son) treats me." I ask, "Why not?" Typically, the reply is "I just knew better." I call it the "perception of authority." When children are convinced that a parent will act resolutely if need be, they will seldom test that parent. Mom's or Dad's authority, therefore, needn't be continually reinforced. It is understood.

It's a simple discipline truth: The will to discipline lessens the need to discipline. What's more, confidence leads to kindness. If a parent repeatedly tries to avoid disciplining, eventually he becomes frustrated and is prone to overreact. Strong discipline isn't loud; it is quietly definite.

To reinforce your authority, here are a few basics:

1. **Use fewer words.** As one expert says, "Act, don't yak."

2. **If you say it, mean it.** And be ready to back it up.

3. **Act early in the chain of misconduct.** Don't allow twenty minutes of mutual irritation to build before you discipline.

4. Employ the three Cs: calm, consistency, consequences.

"Love your kids enough to say no when needed.
Yes can sometimes be the coward's way out."
BETTY (A MOTHER OF TWO IN MISSOURI)

Discipline — Simple Stuff

Good discipline isn't fancy. You don't need a twenty-four-level smiley-face chart, complete with flashing lights, audio-recorded compliments, and a forty-two-page catalog of rewards (probation officers not included). You can do all this if you choose. But effective discipline begins with easy-to-remember and easy-to-enforce consequences.

Parents confess to me, "I can't think of consequences as fast as he can misbehave. Sometimes I even forget what his punishment was." What parents need are some simple consequences that are useful for a wide range of trouble and a wide range of kids.

For preschoolers, use isolation — not from love, but from the scene of the trouble — somewhere in the house, not in the Arctic. My preference: the corner. Most rooms have at least four. A corner is boring; it allows for no panoramic view of the action, as do the steps or couch. For how long? That depends upon the child's age, the seriousness of the infraction, and his willingness to stay put quietly. Some experts' rule of thumb: one minute of time-out for each year of age. Or is it one year per minute of age? I get that one confused.

One minute for each year of age is a classic example of watered-down discipline. Most 4-year-olds aren't even done screaming at the four-minute mark. Moreover, what message is sent to the child who just smacked his sister in the head? "Go to the corner for four minutes. Your sister's head is worth four minutes." Most parents have the good sense to gauge an appropriate amount of corner time.

When is the corner outgrown? Your call, but a colleague of mine still suggests it for preadolescents. Once a child's head is bumping the ceiling, though, you might want to retire the corner. It's hard enough to clean smudges off the walls.

For those kids past preschool, an adaptable consequence is some form of writing. For example, if Harmony is disrespectful, require a four-hundred-word essay on respect — respectfully written, of course (otherwise, you've merely traded slander for libel). Or how about one hundred sentences of "I will keep my rolling eyes to myself." The length and composition of the sentences are based upon your intent and creativity. Or have Oxford define fifteen dictionary words, all of which contain ten or more letters, and use each one in a sentence. After all, if he has to talk crudely, he must need a bigger vocabulary.

Writing has many advantages. It can be beautifully targeted to the offense. It can be completed anywhere, pretty much anytime. It is an automatic denial of privileges. A young-

Have Oxford define fifteen dictionary words, all of which contain ten or more letters, and use each one in a sentence. After all, if he has to talk crudely, he must need a bigger vocabulary.

ster can't be doing much of anything else while he's thinking and writing about his conduct.

"But what if they won't take the discipline?" — a reaction common in many homes, and a sad reflection of the big person's overall loss of authority. All kids misbehave — lots. Such is standard "kidhood." But when a child resists or refuses discipline, his misbehavior moves to another level. It becomes a deliberate, willful challenge to the parent's authority. And it must be directly, firmly addressed.

A strong response to outright defiance is a technique I call "blackout." "Blackout" is complete cessation of all perks and privileges — except love, some kinds of food, and okay, the bathroom. Once a youngster resists the consequence — via arguing, temper fitting, badgering, ignoring, making family life miserable for all — blackout begins. All toys, activities, forms of entertainment, dessert, money supply, transportation, social movement, and whatever else you consider perks cease. Until when? Until you get your initial consequences, with respect and pleasant compliance.

Blackout can also be a consequence in itself for misbehavior you consider particularly serious or defiant: violence, name-calling, temper eruptions, flagrant disrespect, lying, nastiness. Sounds like a promo for an upcoming reality show, doesn't it?

Blackout is a powerful way to clearly assert the authority that must be yours, for the sake of the child and all the family. If you use it resolutely, you won't use it much.

Strong discipline, wrapped in love, not only shapes morals; it is ultimately kind. It leads to less discipline now, and a whole lot less discipline later in life.

Take Away

Discipline is truly one of the very best gifts you can give a child.

CHAPTER 4

It's About Respect

A nationwide survey asked strong families to share their top house rules. Heading the list was "Respect." It was the most often cited and the most firmly enforced. It was nonnegotiable, whether adult to child, child to adult, child to child, or adult to adult.

The families' rationale was indisputable. Respect is an absolute for a healthy relationship. It says, "You have dignity as a person, and I will treat you so." If present, respect can soothe a range of trouble spots. Its absence aggravates those trouble spots and promotes conflicts all its own.

If present, respect can soothe a range of trouble spots. Its absence aggravates those trouble spots and promotes conflicts all its own.

It is critical, therefore, to expect and, where possible, require respect. Mistreatment of another corrodes the relationship. The parent-child bond is unconditional, and the sibling bond is durable, but a relentless verbal battering can take a toll on the sturdiest of emotional ties.

Put simply: *Respect is a manifest form of love. And love is the core of relationships.*

The "Battered Parent Syndrome"

A principle of wise parenting says: Reward the good more, and you'll punish the bad less. However, many experts no longer talk "good" or "bad." That's too judgmental. They substitute morally antisepticised words, such as "appropriate" and "unacceptable." I don't think that's good.

To reward the good more, however, you do have to notice it. Much of my early education focused on helping parents to "catch a child acting good." The idea was that many parents are too focused on misconduct and not enough on best conduct. Nevertheless, the converse, I've come to notice, may be more of a problem, especially for the better parents. They're good at pointing out positives, but they overlook much that is negative, especially in the realm of respect. They allow words, tone, looks, and body language dripping with disdain or disgust. When I ask them how their own parents would have reacted to such conduct, more often than not I hear something like this: "Oh, I never acted that way because I just knew better" or

"That's not something I want to think about" or "I learned really early not to talk like that. It was a line I seldom crossed, even as a teenager."

What was the difference between then and now? The answer is obviously complex; but one factor, I believe, was a much clearer emphasis — spoken and unspoken — on respect. And for most, it wasn't a "You'll act right, kid, because I'm the boss, and I don't want to hear any of your thoughts or opinions." It was more an understood operating principle: This is how we treat one another. And reiterating an idea from the last chapter: The better that kids treat parents, the easier it is for parents to treat kids well. Disrespect from child to parent provokes the same from parent to child.

Many parents nowadays are vexed by what I call the "Battered Parent Syndrome." Inch by inch, they've grown so accustomed to their kids' ugly commentary — verbal and facial — that much of it no longer registers. It's come to be just the way they interact. Only the more hurtful or nasty stuff spurs the parent into some kind of disciplinary reaction.

So the first step toward promoting an overall respectful family environment is to become more sensitive to what is indeed disrespect, to lower

Get better at noticing the bad, and you'll receive more good.

your threshold for what is permissible and what isn't. To put it another way: Get better at noticing the bad, and you'll receive more good.

Expression or Suppression?

The lyrics to the old (1970) song "Express Yourself" can be summed up very simply: Be authentic. Let your honest feelings show.

Experts proclaim, "Feelings are authentic." They are the vital partners of one's thoughts. Therefore, parents especially must be sensitive to allowing a child liberal articulation of his objections, discontent, or opinion. Otherwise, they risk psychologically stunting him.

A guiding axiom in past generations was "A child should be seen and not heard." Most would now consider this extreme, leading some to overcompensate with the other extreme: "A child should be heard, and heard, and heard." Parents now wrestle with the anxiety that a strong stance against disrespect risks raising a robotic "Stepford" child, who truly feels but won't express: "Yes, Mother, I will obey you, but down deep I can't stand you."

What's a parent to do? On the one hand, we want to be open to youngsters' viewpoints, especially when they disagree with us, which is about 76.27

percent of the time. On the other hand, kids can get pretty ill-mannered or downright snotty when offering their viewpoints. Does suppressing disrespect automatically stifle freedom of speech? Not in the least. Requiring respect enhances communication. Without a governor on them, feelings can become abusive. And few people can endure a nasty barrage for very long without becoming reciprocally nasty. Perhaps Mother Teresa could, but she wasn't a parent, and she only worked with the most destitute on the mean streets of Calcutta. She never had to engage and persuade a 14-year-old about why she can't sleep overnight at the mall.

To complicate matters, a parent can struggle over where to draw the line separating legitimate expression from illegitimate disrespect.

Mother Teresa never had to engage and persuade a 14-year-old about why she can't sleep overnight at the mall.

Here's an experiment to help. Imagine that your best friend is talking and acting toward you like your youngster sometimes does. How would that affect your relationship? How many peevish remarks, rolling eyes, and "Whatevers" could you withstand before you reacted with this: "I do so appreciate your authenticity. It makes you much more likeably genuine, but I am beginning to feel a smidgen demeaned"? Yeah, right.

Conduct that's wrong adult to adult is likewise wrong child to adult, adult to child, and child to child. How about a house rule? *Expression is fully free until any kind of disrespect intrudes.* At that point, the expresser forfeits the right to be heard, temporarily, with consequences enforced by the parent, if judged necessary. A youngster has the inalienable right to speak, as long as he controls his emotions, words, tone, and body language. In short, anything — verbal or nonverbal — that mistreats another family member is prohibited. The license to express carries with it the responsibility to express respectfully.

"There is a difference between disrespectful back talk and respectful discussion, usually apparent in tone and attitude. Sometimes it's a thin line, and I don't always guess right."
JERRY (A FATHER OF FOUR IN OREGON)

Honor Thy Teacher and Coach?

Parents commonly lean on a consolation that goes something like this: "She's (or He's) got a real attitude with me. She's surly and likes to argue. But everybody else says she's a great kid. They love her at school. So I guess I should be pleased."

Well, yes and no. We shrinks are trained to give straight answers. Yes, it's good that she's pleasant and respectful with others. She has internalized some social graces. No, it's not good that she reserves her disagreeable conduct for her mother, father, or both. Granted, kids typically are more secure in their parents' love, so with us they may act at their relaxed worst. Nevertheless, parents deserve the highest level of respect. A mother and father have such inherent dignity that God gave them 10 percent of His commandments. He mentioned them specifically by name, along with the word "honor."

Let's conduct a field test. Moms, you will be our subjects. Suppose a woman approaches you somewhere out in public, saying, "You don't know me, but I work with your husband. And I have to tell you, he is one of the most pleasant people I know. He always has a kind word for everyone, and I don't think I've ever seen him irritated." Now, if that describes him at home, you might concur: "Thank you. Yes, he is a great husband and father." But if he's not so positive with you and the family, you might muster a faint smile, along with a forced "Thank you" of sorts.

What were meant as compliments would sting. They would remind you that on the respect pyramid, you're not always at the top. Because you are not responsible for raising your spouse — well, not totally, anyway — you can't directly require, under penalty of discipline, his respect. But you are directly responsible for raising respectful, morally mature children. And the foremost place they'll learn is at home with the family.

Some years ago, my wife, Randi, gave our then 12-year-old daughter, Sarah, two hours of "labor." In our home, "labor" means being assigned multiple chores for a specified time, with no bad attitude or put-upon victim status permitted. Otherwise, the original time is extended. When I asked Randi how Sarah earned two full labor hours, she replied: "She rolled her eyes at me." Two hours of work for rolling her eyes?! Is that because eye rolling is so awful? No, it's because a mother is so valuable. A strong message needed to be sent.

Did Sarah ever roll her eyes again? Did McDonald's ever sell another hamburger? But in the past several years, we have gotten the family room remodeled, the garage painted, the shed reroofed, and the dishes washed 374 times.

"When [back talk] occurred, we ceased dealing with any issue other than the rudeness. Later, we discussed the problem that provoked the back talk."
PAT (MOTHER TO FIVE CHILDREN AND DOZENS OF FOSTER CHILDREN IN NEW JERSEY)

Good Consequences for Bad Words

Perhaps you need little convincing to take a strong stand for respect — though you may be like many, in whom the spirit is willing, but the flesh has gotten flabby. Over time, you may have slipped in your standards a bit. You've realized that as "nice a kid as everyone thinks he is," you would do well to make him even nicer, particularly toward you.

So how do you enforce your expectations? As with any discipline, you need consequences — clear, firm, and repeatable. Furthermore, your consequences need to match your standards. If you highly value respect, make your response say so. Here is a menu of options:

1. **An automatic twenty-four-hour grounding from the spot of the foul.** Or depending upon the seriousness of the offense, a twenty-four-hour blackout. If trouble occurs within the twenty-four hours, reset the clock.

2. **A writing assignment:** (a) Compose an essay on respect — length depending upon age and infraction. (b) Copy sentences about respect — ten or more. (c) List twenty-five nice qualities about the person disrespected. (d) Compose twenty-five reasons why it's a blessing to live in the family. (e) Find

and define ten synonyms for "respect"; use them in sentences containing the name of the person mistreated.

3. **Labor — chores over time.** How many? How long? Use your judgment, based on the type of disrespect, duration, and ultimate contrition.

4. **Physical activity.** Push-ups, sit-ups, or laps around the house or yard. Moving a stack of something to another place, and then back if need be.

5. **Become a servant for the person offended.** Time is again set by seriousness of the infraction.

6. **Immediate loss of the most valued privilege, activity, or possession for the day.** Make it longer if disrespectful resistance is displayed.

7. **Serve time in a corner, in a room, or on the steps — quietly.** Time served for disrespect is longer than for most other misconduct.

> *"Back talk, when it does sneak into the conversation, is pointed out as showing a lack of respect, and if not stopped at once, consequences . . . are used."*
> GARY AND MARGE (PARENTS OF TWO TEENS IN FORT COLLINS, COLORADO)

Last Respects

Implementing a zero-tolerance approach toward disrespect in any form — back talk, dirty looks, surly debating, disdainful body language — is not an autocratic parental show of mind control. It is simply establishing a legitimately high standard, one that fewer parents are reaching for.

Requiring respect does not stifle a child's thoughts and feelings. In fact, it gives them a wide avenue. It likewise does not create an emotional automaton — cooperative on the outside, hostile on the inside. Instead, it eliminates an ugly habit or keeps one from forming. Put simply, fewer bad expressions allow more good expressions.

Take Away

Requiring respect is a family basic, not an optional extra.

CHAPTER 5

The Moral Question

What makes good families good? That was the question driving a nationwide search for quality families. The resulting book, *Back to the Family* (which I authored with David Eich), revealed a dominant theme: spiritual faith, or "the belief in a Creator and in living by His guidelines."

A mother once asked me, "Do you need religion to raise a great kid?" I answered with a question (we shrinks do that): "How will you decide what to teach?" If it is Mom and Dad's ideas of "how to live well," could the child not one day legitimately argue: "You have your morals, and I have mine. Yours work for you, but not for me." It's a logical rebuttal.

Of course, any parent can hear something similar from any child, particularly from a young adult. There is, however, an undeniable difference between "These are my personal standards" and "These are the standards of an all-wise, infinite Being." Someone can reject either, but God knows far better than parents — or, for that matter, kids — the best way to live.

The award-winning teachers who identified the "best we've seen" families based their judgment upon the character of the children in the families. Interviews revealed the foundation for that character: the presence of a religiously based sensibility guiding family life. Agree or disagree on its importance, but that's what, in fact, emerged. Great kids most often grow from strong morals taught and practiced by faithful parents.

"I don't think religion has made us a success as a family, but as individual human beings. Being successful humans makes you a successful family."
KATY (AGE 15)

Raise Your Bar

Regularly, I will ask a parent: "Do you want to raise an average child, one who morally is pretty much the norm out there? Or do you want to raise an exemplary child, one who clearly lives above the crowd in his morals?" I do recall one mom back in 1981 choosing the average option.

To be sure, the real-life implications of raising an "abnormal" child are far-reaching. Your expectations for good conduct will be higher than many, if not most, around you. You will require respect, cooperation, and responsibility well above that practiced by your child's age group. You will supervise his whereabouts, entertainment, and peer choices far more closely than other parents do. You will allow social freedoms two, three, and four years later than his peers routinely get them.

And for it all, you will be misunderstood and second-guessed, not only by your kids — you can expect that — but also by other adults. Some of the most disapproving feedback for your "parenting extremes" will come from friends, relatives, and pop-psychology notions.

As one who has been "shrinking" for over thirty years — I used to be 6 feet 9 inches — I've watched good parents navigate a culture progressively more hostile to their values. If you stand strong, I can almost guarantee what you'll hear in time from those same critical commentators: "You've got great kids." Then again, you may still not get credit: "You're so lucky. You've just got good kids. You have Chastity and Angelica. I didn't get good kids. I got Chucky, Damien, and Cujo."

In the end, reality always wins. The proof of your out-of-the-norm parenting will be apparent in the above-the-norm quality of the adults you give to this world.

> *"I would want my kids to always stand up and face the wind. [It's] a reflection of the strength that is often required of people to maintain themselves in our society today."*
> JAY (A FATHER IN ARIZONA)

Walk the Talk?

Be a good model, and your kids will follow. Values are caught, not taught. Children learn what they see. Show, don't tell. All of these axioms emphasize the central role of being a good example. Nobody would argue that it's not dramatically easier to raise kids well if you yourself are striving to live well. Nevertheless, like many child-rearing guidelines, teaching by example will take you only so far. To begin, it assumes little Echo is an observant student. It assumes she has the willingness to imitate. In essence, it assumes she is a little adult.

No matter how flawless your role modeling, a child doesn't have the self-control or maturity to always mirror your lead. He will stumble regularly — indeed, don't we all? — mainly because of who he is: a child. He can't be expected to be grown up just because you are. And when he's not, you must teach him, or discipline him, or restrict him. In other words, teaching morals has to be both passive and active.

A 36-year-old mother came to me with several complaints about her 12-year-old son: he watches too much television, he eats too much, and he's lazy. After digging to the bottom of why Mom allowed this for years, the short answer was "I watch too much television, I eat too much, and I'm lazy."

I asked, "Do you want your son to be just like you?"

"Of course not," she said.

"Then you'll have to take charge of his habits, though you yourself don't have the self-discipline to conquer your habits."

If you smoke, is it then permissible for your 16-year-old to smoke? If coarse words accompany your temper outbursts, will you allow your 8-year-old his own eruptions and nastiness if he gets upset enough? In short, will you accept bad behavior from your children because you yourself do the same?

In all manner of ways — the most crucial being character — I want my children to be better than I am. Therefore, I am forced to require standards for them that I might not fully have reached. To the extent that I relentlessly work on my own moral conduct, I will have more credibility and authority in their eyes. But for their sake, I can't use myself as the standard-bearer, since I'm not yet where I'd like them to someday be.

If coarse words accompany your temper outbursts, will you allow your 8-year-old his own eruptions and nastiness?

Yes, walk the talk. But know that the God-given duty to teach is not founded upon our own moral superiority. If it were, we'd all be in trouble.

Know Your Competition

Parents routinely are bewildered by the teen sitting across from them in my office. In so many words, their lament is: "I don't know who that is. What made him get this way? It's not how I raised him." Often I can say, "I believe you. But you may have underestimated the power of what did."

Never in human history have parents had to battle forces that daily can enter their very homes, live among them, and relentlessly manipulate how their children think and behave. These forces are formidable, soul shaping, and seductive. The parents' main defense against them is vigilance — awareness of what they are and how they work — and a determined willingness to reduce or prevent access to their children.

For better or worse, the technological advances affecting our families are here to stay. What's more, they are on fast-forward. Thus, it is all the more imperative that parents realize what they are confronting. Otherwise, beneath their radar, attitudes, desires, and morals will be molded that are dramatically counter to those the parents are trying to instill.

Here are some fundamental suggestions to control the competition:

1. **Install the most advanced filter system for your computer.** The computer is a gate to the world's playground, full of both good and evil. Even if your child doesn't seek the bad, it will seek him if you let it. Set up a password to limit access to times of your choosing. Do *not* put a computer in a child's bedroom. Public placement is the best placement. Do not assume that the parents of your child's friends practice technology vigilance similar to yours.

2. **Even though it seems most preschoolers will soon carry cell phones, consider waiting until late high school or college.** Cell phones provide

fast and wide social connections, healthy and otherwise. Kids gravitate toward the digital, which pushes aside the personal, most often meaning parents and siblings. Concerned about safety and schedule? Purchase a phone with a monthly ten-minute limit, programmed to send and receive select numbers.

3. **Curtail video/computer games, eliminating any with remotely objectionable content.** They are sirens in their appeal, stealing from more valuable things: schoolwork, reading, visiting, playing, and even being just plain bored (downtime).

4. **Limit and strictly monitor the eye and ear junk food.** If your child has no television in his room, he is now in the American-kid minority. It isn't only the rampant immorality that TV can stuff into your child's head; it's a whole package of thinking and feeling about life, most of which I'm sure you don't agree with at all.

5. **Slow the pace of social freedom.** The typical youngster is racing into the social/romantic/ entertainment scene at a pace overwhelming her level of emotional and moral maturity. Don't use the peer group as a guide to what is the norm. When in doubt, delay.

Even if your child doesn't seek the bad, it will seek him if you let it.

I suspect you're not about to move to a remote cabin in northern Canada. Nor do you need to. Nevertheless, wise parents constantly fine-tune their awareness of what is lurking to raise their child. Even wiser parents stand strong to protect, supervise, and defeat any unwanted, morally warping competition.

> *"Our expert is our Heavenly Father. We continually pray for His guidance for each child.... We listen and try to follow."*
> ROSS AND JULIE (PARENTS OF FOUR IN UTAH)

Pray Tell

There's a child-rearing axiom: From birth to age 6, you teach children; from ages 6 to 12, you guide them; from 12 to 18, you pray for them. Perhaps this is a bit of an oversimplification. Teaching and guiding seldom ever completely cease. And many parents pray from the day the child enters their world until the day they leave his. They believe that a loving Creator is in charge of this universe, so seeking His help and input makes perfect sense.

Commonly, a person of faith will call my radio program with a parenting question. Shortly thereafter, someone else may call to advise me that I should have encouraged the caller to pray about her situation. I respond that, no doubt, as a religious person, she's been doing so all along. I wouldn't suspect I'd hear, "Thanks, Dr. Ray. I've never even thought of prayer."

Further, it's obvious to me that many parents pray, not only during times of trouble, but also regularly and spontaneously throughout the day – bedtime, mealtime, and prior to trips and sporting events. Dropping off a child at school, they drop off a little prayer with him. They ask God to ease conflicts, anxiety, or struggles with a friend. In essence, they show the kids that a caring God is waiting and willing to listen, and wants to walk alongside the family.

Suppose I were to offer you a free dinner, a free vacation, or free money with no conditions. All you'd have to do is ask. It's likely you'd jump at my offer before I was finished speaking – not from selfishness or greed, but from recognizing a good thing. Prayer is a good thing. It is access to guidance and peace far beyond the value of free dinners or money. Prayer costs nothing.

The ultimate Expert knows your family better than you or I do. Tap into His limitless reservoir of understanding.

Yet its return, for your family and your life, is immeasurable. Experts like myself can provide some useful parenting direction. But the ultimate Expert knows your family better than you or I do. Tap into His limitless reservoir of understanding.

Praying to an all-wise, all-knowing Being isn't self-serving. It is very, very smart. I'd say that it's smarter than doing rocket science.

Take Away

Set high moral standards, model them, enforce them — and pray.

ABOUT THE AUTHOR

DR. RAY GUARENDI, a father of ten, is a clinical psychologist, author, public speaker, and radio host. His radio show — "The Doctor Is In" — can be heard weekdays on both Ave Maria Radio and EWTN Radio affiliates.

Dr. Guarendi's experience includes working in school districts, Head Start programs, mental health centers, substance abuse programs, inpatient psychiatric centers, juvenile courts, and a private practice.

Dr. Guarendi has been a regular guest on national radio and television programs, including *Oprah*, *Joan Rivers*, *Scott Ross Prime Time*, *700 Club*, and *CBS This Morning*. He has appeared on regional radio and television shows in over forty states and Canada. He has been the program psychologist for Cleveland's *Morning Exchange*, *Pittsburgh 2Day*, and *AM Indiana*. He has written several books, including **Discipline That Lasts a Lifetime; You're a Better Parent Than You Think** (now in its twenty-eighth printing); **Back to the Family; Good Discipline, Great Teens**; and his newest book, **Adoption: Choosing It, Living It, Loving It**.